The Ultimate

Tasty and Easy to

Ann Newman

Table of Contents

Introduction

Air-fried foods have a lower fat content than fried foods, which means they are healthier.

The Air Fryer has the following benefits, such as: weight loss, air fryers can be safer than classic fryers and reduce the risk of toxic acrylamide formation, and crucially reduces the risk of disease!

Alternatively, you can use the Ninja Foodi.

The Ninja Foodi grill is a new way to enjoy grill food indoor, which is prepared straight in the kitchen and served to your dining tables.

If you love the grill and perfectly chard food that is unique, delicious, and easy to prepare then the Ninja Foodi grill offers a quick-cooking style and makes every meal a special treat and gives a fresh vibe to the food.

This cookbook series covers some astonishing recipes that are prepared using Air Fryer and also Ninja Foodi grill using some of the best whole, hearty, and healthy ingredients. All the recipes are created by adding some extra twist to them.

Before getting toward the recipe part, it is very important to get to know about the air fryer and the grill, their functions, and tip and trick to maintain and use the appliance.

The meals that are introduced in this book are targeted towards all the family members, includes everything from breakfast, lunch, snacks, dessert, to mouthwatering dinners. Enjoy!

1. Banana Bread

Preparation Time 10 m
Cooking Time 20 m
8 Serves

Ingredients:

- 3 bananas, peeled and sliced
- 1 teaspoon ground cinnamon
- ½ cup olive oil
- 1 1/3 cups flour
- 2/3 cup sugar
- 1 teaspoon baking soda

- 1 teaspoon baking powder
- ¼ teaspoon salt
- ½ cup milk

Method:

In the bowl of a stand mixer, add all the ingredients and mix until well combined. Place the mixture into a greased loaf pan. Arrange the "Crisper Basket" in the pot of Ninja Foodi Grill. Close the Ninja Foodi Grill with lid and select "Air Crisp". Set the temperature to 330 degrees F to preheat. Press "Start/Stop" to begin preheating. When the display shows "Add Food" open the lid and place the loaf pan into the "Crisper Basket". Close the Ninja Foodi Grill with lid and set the time for 20 minutes. Press "Start/Stop" to begin cooking. When the cooking time is completed, press "Start/Stop" to stop cooking and open the lid. Place the pan onto a wire rack for about 10 minutes. Carefully invert the bread onto the wire rack to cool completely before slicing. Cut the bread into desired sized slices and serve. Enjoy!

Nutrition:

Calories: 295
Fat: 13.3g
Saturated Fat: 2.1g
Carbs: 44g
Sugar: 22.8g
Protein: 3.1g

2. Sweet Potato Frittata

Preparation Time 10 m
Cooking Time 30 m
6 Serves

Ingredients:

- Salt
- 1 sweet potato, diced
- Pepper
- 10 eggs
- 1/4 cup goat cheese, crumbled
- 1 onion, diced
- 2 cups broccoli, chopped
- 1 tbsp. olive oil

Method:
Spray a baking dish using cooking spray and set aside. Insert wire rack in rack position 6. Select bake, set temperature 390 F, timer for 20 minutes. Press start to preheat the oven. Heat oil in a pan over medium heat. Add sweet potato, broccoli, and onion and cook for 10-15 minutes or until sweet potato is tender. In a large bowl, whisk eggs with pepper and salt. Transfer cooked vegetables into the baking dish. Pour egg mixture over vegetables. Spray in goat cheese and bake for 15-20 minutes. Slice and serve. Enjoy!

Nutrition:
Calories 201

Fat 13 g
Carbs 8.4 g
Sugar 3.3 g
Protein 13.5 g
Cholesterol 282 mg

3. Quick Cheese Omelet

Preparation Time 5 m
Cooking Time 9 m
1 Serves

Ingredients:

- Salt
- ¼ cup cheddar cheese, shredded
- Pepper
- 2 eggs, lightly beaten
- ¼ cup milk

Method:
In a bowl, whisk milk, eggs with pepper, and salt. Spray small air fryer pan with cooking spray. Pour egg mixture into the prepared pan and cook at 350 F for 6 minutes. Sprinkle cheese on top and cook for 3 minutes more. Serve. Enjoy!

Nutrition:
Calories 270
Fat 19.4 g
Carbs 4.1 g
Sugar 3.6 g
Protein 20.1 g
Cholesterol 362 mg

4. Savory French Toast

Preparation Time 10 m
Cooking Time 5 m
2 Serves

Ingredients:

- 4 bread slices
- 2 teaspoons green chili, seeded and finely chopped
- Water, as needed
- ¼ cup chickpea flour
- 3 tablespoons onion, finely chopped
- ½ teaspoon red chili powder
- ¼ teaspoon ground turmeric
- ¼ teaspoon ground cumin
- Salt, to taste

Method:
Add all the ingredients except bread slices in a large bowl and mix until a thick mixture form. With a spoon, spread the mixture over both sides of each bread slice. Arrange the bread slices into the lightly greased the sheet pan. Press "Power Button" of Air Fry Oven and turn the dial to select the "Air Fry" mode. Press the Time button and again turn the dial to set the cooking time to 5 minutes. Now push the Temp button and rotate the dial to set the temperature at 390 degrees F. Press "Start/Pause" button to start. When the unit beeps to show that it is preheated, open the lid and lightly, grease sheet pan. Arrange the bread slices into "Air Fry Basket" and insert in the oven. Flip the bread slices

once halfway through. Serve warm. Enjoy!

Nutrition:
Calories 151
Fat 2.3 g
Cholesterol 0 mg
Sodium 234 mg
Carbs 26.7 g
Fiber 5.4 g
Protein 6.5g

5. Mushroom & Pepperoncini Omelet

Preparation Time 15 m
Cooking Time 20 m
2 Serves

Ingredients:

- ½ tablespoon scallion, sliced thinly
- ½ cup cheddar cheese, shredded
- 3 pepperoncini peppers, sliced thinly
- 3 large eggs
- ¼ c milk
- Salt and ground black pepper, as required
- ¼ cup cooked mushrooms

Method:
In a bowl, add the eggs, milk, salt and black pepper and beat well. Place the mixture into a greased baking pan. Press "Power Button" of Air Fry Oven and turn the dial to select the "Air Bake" mode. Press the Time button and again turn the dial to set the cooking time to 20 minutes. Now push the Temp button and rotate the dial to set the temperature at 350 degrees F. Press "Start/Pause" button to start. When the unit beeps to show that it is preheated, open the lid. Arrange pan over the "Wire Rack" and insert in the oven. Cut into equal-sized wedges and serve hot. Enjoy!

Nutrition:
Calories 254

Fat 17.5 g
Cholesterol 311 mg
Sodium 793 mg
Carbs 7.3 g
Fiber 0.1 g
Protein 8.2 g

6. Mushroom Frittata

Preparation Time 15 m
Cooking Time 36 m
4 Serves

Ingredients:

- ½ cup cream cheese, softened
- 4 cups white mushrooms, chopped
- ½ teaspoon fresh dill, minced
- 2 tablespoons olive oil
- 1 shallot, sliced thinly
- 2 garlic cloves, minced

- 6 large eggs
- ¼ teaspoon red pepper flakes, crushed
- Salt and ground black pepper, as required

Method:

In a skillet, heat the oil over medium heat and cook the shallot, mushrooms and garlic for about 5-6 minutes, stirring frequently. Remove from the heat and transfer the mushroom mixture into a bowl. In another bowl, add the eggs, red pepper flakes, salt and black peppers and beat well. Add the mushroom mixture and stir to combine. Place the egg mixture into a greased baking pan and sprinkle with the dill. Spread cream cheese over egg mixture evenly. Press "Power Button" of Air Fry Oven and turn the dial to select the "Air Fry" mode. Press the Time button and again turn the dial to set the cooking time to 30 minutes. Now push the Temp button and rotate the dial to set the temperature at 330 degrees F. Press "Start/Pause" button to start. When the unit beeps to show that it is preheated, open the lid. Arrange pan over the "Wire Rack" and insert in the oven. Cut into equal-sized wedges and serve. Enjoy!

Nutrition:
Calories 290
Fat 24.8g
Cholesterol 311 mg
Sodium 236 mg
Carbs 5 g
Fiber 0.8 g
Protein 14.1 g

7. Chicken & Broccoli Quiche

Preparation Time 15 m
Cooking Time 12 m
2 Serves

Ingredients:

- 2 tablespoons cooked chicken, chopped
- 1 small egg
- 3 tablespoons boiled broccoli, chopped
- ½ of frozen ready-made pie crust
- ¼ tablespoon olive oil
- 3 tablespoons cheddar cheese, grated
- 1½ tablespoons whipping cream
- Salt and freshly ground black pepper, as needed

Method:
Cut 1 (5-inch) round from the pie crust. Arrange the pie crust round in a small pie pan and gently, press in the bottom and sides. In a bowl, mix together the egg, cheese, cream, salt, and black pepper. Pour the egg mixture over dough base and top with the broccoli and chicken. Press "Power Button" of Air Fry Oven and turn the dial to select the "Air Fry" mode. Press the Time button and again turn the dial to set the cooking time to 12 minutes. Now push the Temp button and rotate the dial to set the temperature at 390 degrees F. Press "Start/Pause" button to start. When the unit beeps to show that it is preheated, open the lid. Arrange pan over the "Wire Rack" and insert in the oven. Cut into equal-sized wedges and serve. Enjoy!

Nutrition:
Calories 197
Fat 15 g
Cholesterol 99 mg
Sodium 184 mg
Carbs 7.4 g
Fiber 0.4 g
Protein 8.6 g

8. Eggs in Bread & Sausage Cups

Preparation Time 10 m
Cooking Time 22 m
2 Serves

Ingredients:

- ¼ cup mozzarella cheese, grated
- 2 cooked sausages, sliced
- ¼ cup cream
- 3 eggs
- 1 bread slice, cut into sticks

Method:

In a bowl, add the cream and eggs and beat well. Transfer the egg mixture into ramekins. Place the sausage slices and bread sticks around the edges and gently push them in the egg mixture. Sprinkle with the cheese evenly. Press "Power Button" of Air Fry Oven and turn the dial to select the "Air Fry" mode. Press the Time button and again turn the dial to set the cooking time to 22 minutes. Now push the Temp button and rotate the dial to set the temperature at 355 degrees F. Press "Start/Pause" button to start. When the unit beeps to show that it is preheated, open the lid. Arrange the ramekins over the "Wire Rack" and insert in the oven. Serve warm. Enjoy!

Nutrition:
Calories 229
Fat 18.6 g

Cholesterol 278 mg
Sodium 360 mg
Carbs 3.9 g
Fiber 0.1g
Protein 15.2 g

9. Bacon & Spinach Quiche

Preparation Time 15 m
Cooking Time 10 m
4 Serves

Ingredients:

- Salt and ground black pepper, as required
- ¼ cup mozzarella cheese, shredded
- 2 dashes Tabasco sauce
- 2 cooked bacon slices, chopped
- ½ cup fresh spinach, chopped
- ½ cup Parmesan cheese, shredded
- 2 tablespoons milk

Method:
In a bowl, add all ingredients and mix well. Transfer the mixture into a baking pan. Press "Power Button" of Air Fry Oven and turn the dial to select the "Air Fry" mode. Press the Time button and again turn the dial to set the cooking time to 10 minutes. Now push the Temp button and rotate the dial to set the temperature at 320 degrees F. Press "Start/Pause" button to start. When the unit beeps to show that it is preheated, open the lid. Arrange pan over the "Wire Rack" and insert in the oven. Enjoy!

Nutrition:
Calories 130
Fat 9.3 g

Cholesterol 25 mg
Sodium 561 mg
Carbs 1.1 g
Fiber 0.1 g
Protein 10 g

10. Coconut Blueberry Oatmeal

Preparation Time 10 m
Cooking Time 30 m
6 Serves

Ingredients:

- 1/8 tsp salt
- 1/2 tsp vanilla
- 6 tbsp. brown sugar
- 2 1/4 cups oats

- 1 cup blueberries
- 1/4 cup gluten-free flour
- 3 cups of water
- 14 oz. coconut milk

Method:
Add all ingredients into the instant pot and stir well. Seal pot with lid and cook on manual mode for 30 minutes. Once done then release pressure using the quick-release method than open the lid. Stir well and serve. Enjoy!

Nutrition:
Calories 337
Fat 18.1 g
Carbs 40.3 g
Sugar 13.7 g
Protein 6.4 g
Cholesterol 0 mg

11. Coconut Lime Breakfast Quinoa

Preparation Time 10 m
Cooking Time 1 m
5 Serves

Ingredients:

- 1 cup of water
- 1 lime juice
- 2 cups of coconut milk
- 1 cup quinoa, rinsed
- 1/2 tsp coconut extract
- 1 lime zest

Method:
Add all ingredients into the instant pot and stir well. Seal pot with lid and cook on manual high pressure for 1 minute. Once done then allow to release pressure naturally for 10 minutes then release using the quick-release method. Open the lid. Stir well and serve. Enjoy!

Nutrition:
Calories 350
Fat 25 g
Carbs 28.1 g
Sugar 3.5 g
Protein 7.1 g
Cholesterol 0 mg

12. Egg Paprika Scramble

Preparation Time 10 m
Cooking Time 10 m
6 Serves

Ingredients:

- Two teaspoons sweet paprika
- Salt and black pepper to taste
- Four eggs whisked
- A drizzle olive oil
- One red onion, chopped

Method:
Add everything to a suitably sized bowl and stir well. Add this prepared mixture to the Instant Pot. Put on the Instant Air Fryer lid and cook on Bake mode for 10 minutes at 200 degrees F. Once done, remove the lid and serve warm. Enjoy!

Nutrition:
Calories: 190
Protein: 4g
Carbs: 12g
Fat: 7g

13. Cauliflower Mash

Preparation Time 10 m
Cooking Time 3 m
6 Serves

Ingredients:

- 1/4 tsp salt
- 1/2 tsp garlic powder
- 2 cups vegetable stock
- 1 large cauliflower head, cut into florets
- 1/2 cup parmesan cheese, shredded
- 2 tbsp. butter

Method:

Pour the stock into the instant pot then place a steamer basket into the pot. Add cauliflower florets into the steamer basket. Seal pot with lid and cook on high pressure for 3 minutes. Once done then release pressure using the quick-release method than open the lid. Transfer cauliflower into the food processor along with remaining ingredients and blend until smooth. Serve. Enjoy!

Nutrition:
Calories 102
Fat 6 g
Carbs 8.2 g
Sugar 3.7 g

Protein 6 g
Cholesterol 17 mg

14. Spicy Whole Chicken

Preparation Time 15 m
Cooking Time 1 h
4 Serves

Ingredients:

- Salt and freshly ground black pepper, to taste
- 1 teaspoon ground white pepper
- 3 tablespoons oil
- 2 teaspoons dried thyme
- 2 teaspoons paprika
- 1 teaspoon cayenne pepper
- 1 teaspoon onion powder
- 1 teaspoon garlic powder
- 1 (5-pound) whole chicken, necks and giblets removed

Method:

In a bowl, mix together the thyme and spices. Coat the chicken with oil and then rub it with spice mixture. Season the chicken with salt and black pepper evenly. Arrange the greased "Crisper Basket" in the pot of Ninja Foodi Grill. Close the Ninja Foodi Grill with lid and select "Air Crisp". Set the temperature to 350 degrees F to preheat. Press "Start/Stop" to begin preheating. When the display shows "Add Food" open the lid and place the chicken into the "Crisper Basket". Close the Ninja Foodi Grill with lid and set the time for 1 hour. Press "Start/Stop" to begin cooking. Flip the chicken once after 30 minutes. When cooking time is completed, press "Start/Stop" to stop cooking and open the lid.

Place the chicken onto a cutting board for about 10 minutes before carving. Cut the chicken into desired sized pieces and serve. Enjoy!

Nutrition:
Calories: 590
Fat: 26.3g
Saturated Fat: 6.5g
Carbs: 1.3g
Sugar: 0.3g
Protein: 82.3g

15. Lemony Chicken Thighs

Preparation Time 10 m
Cooking Time 20 m
6 Serves

Ingredients:

- 1 lemon, sliced thinly
- 2 tablespoons fresh lemon juice
- Salt and freshly ground black pepper, to taste
- 6 (6-ounce) chicken thighs

- 2 tablespoons olive oil
- 1 tablespoon Italian seasoning

Method:

In a large bowl, add all the ingredients except for lemon slices and toss to coat well. Refrigerate to marinate for 30 minutes to overnight. Remove the chicken thighs and let any excess marinade drip off. Arrange the "Crisper Basket" in the pot of Ninja Foodi Grill. Close the Ninja Foodi Grill with lid and select "Air Crisp". Set the temperature to 350 degrees F to preheat. Press "Start/Stop" to begin preheating. When the display shows "Add Food" open the lid and place the chicken thighs into the "Crisper Basket". Close the Ninja Foodi Grill with lid and set the time for 20 minutes. Press "Start/Stop" to begin cooking. After 10 minutes of cooking, flip the chicken thighs. When the cooking time is completed, press "Start/Stop" to stop cooking and open the lid. Serve hot alongside the lemon slices. Enjoy!

Nutrition:

Calories: 372

Fat: 18g

Saturated Fat: 4.3g

Carbs: 0.6g

Sugar: 0.4g

Protein: 49.3g

16. Chicken Cordon Bleu

Preparation Time 15 m
Cooking Time 30 m
2 Serves

Ingredients:

- 1 tablespoon butter, melted
- Salt and freshly ground black pepper, to taste
- 1 tablespoon olive oil
- 2 (6-ounce) boneless, skinless chicken breast halves, pounded into ¼-inch thickness
- 2 (¾-ounce) deli ham slices
- 2 Swiss cheese slices
- ½ cup all-purpose flour
- 1/8 teaspoon paprika
- 1 large egg
- 2 tablespoons 2% milk
- ½ cup seasoned breadcrumbs

Method:
Arrange the chicken breast halves onto a smooth surface. Arrange 1 ham slice over each chicken breast half, followed by the cheese. Roll up each chicken breast half and tuck in ends. With toothpicks, secure the rolls. In a shallow plate, mix together the flour, paprika, salt and black pepper. In a shallow bowl, place the egg and milk and beat slightly. In a second shallow plate, place the breadcrumbs. Coat each chicken roll with flour mixture, then dip into egg

mixture and finally coat with breadcrumbs. In a small skillet, heat the oil over medium heat and cook the chicken rolls for about 3-5 minutes or until browned from all sides. Transfer the chicken rolls into the greased baking pan. Arrange the "Crisper Basket" in the pot of Ninja Foodi Grill. Close the Ninja Foodi Grill with lid and select "Bake". Set the temperature to 350 degrees F to preheat. Press "Start/Stop" to begin preheating. When the display shows "Add Food" open the lid and place the pan into the "Crisper Basket". Close the Ninja Foodi Grill with lid and set the time for 25 minutes. Press "Start/Stop" to begin cooking. When the cooking time is completed, press "Start/Stop" to stop cooking and open the lid. Place the chicken rolls onto a platter and discard the toothpicks. Drizzle with melted butter and serve. Enjoy!

Nutrition:
Calories: 672
Fat: 28g
Saturated Fat: 9.3g
Carbs: 45.9g
Sugar: 3.4g
Protein: 56.2g

17. Chicken Kabobs

Preparation Time 15 m
Cooking Time 7 m
3 Serves

Ingredients:

- 1 pound chicken tenders
- 2 tablespoons low-sodium soy sauce
- Pinch of ground black pepper
- 4 scallions, chopped
- 1 tablespoon fresh ginger, finely grated
- 4 garlic cloves, minced
- 2 tablespoons fresh lime juice
- 1 tablespoon olive oil
- 2 teaspoons sugar

Method:

In a large baking pan, mix together the scallion, ginger, garlic, pineapple juice, soy sauce, oil, sesame seeds, and black pepper. Thread chicken tenders onto the pre-soaked wooden skewers. Add the skewers into the baking pan and coat with marinade evenly. Cover and refrigerate for about 2 hours or overnight. Arrange the greased "Crisper Basket" in the pot of Ninja Foodi Grill. Close the Ninja Foodi Grill with lid and select "Air Crisp". Set the temperature to 390 degrees to preheat. Press "Start/Stop" to begin preheating. When the display shows "Add Food" open the lid and place the skewers into the "Crisper Basket". Close the Ninja Foodi Grill with lid and set the time for 7 minutes. Press "Start/Stop" to begin cooking. When the cooking time is completed, press "Start/Stop" to stop cooking and open the lid. Serve hot. Enjoy!

Nutrition:
Calories: 360
Fat: 16g
Saturated Fat: 3.8g
Carbs: 7.5g
Sugar: 3.9g
Protein: 45.2g

18. Simple Turkey Wings

Preparation Time 10 m
Cooking Time 26 m
4 Serves

Ingredients:

- 3 tablespoons olive oil
- 2 pounds turkey wings
- 4 tablespoons chicken rub

Method:
In a large bowl, add the turkey wings, chicken rub and olive oil and toss to coat well. Arrange the greased "Crisper Basket" in the pot of Ninja Foodi Grill. Close the Ninja Foodi Grill with lid and select "Air Crisp". Set the temperature to 380 degrees F to preheat. Press "Start/Stop" to begin preheating. When the display shows "Add Food" open the lid and place the turkey wings into the "Crisper Basket". Close the Ninja Foodi Grill with lid and set the time for 26 minutes. Press "Start/Stop" to begin cooking. Flip the turkey wings once halfway through. When the cooking time is completed, press "Start/Stop" to stop cooking and open the lid. Serve hot. Enjoy!

Nutrition:
Calories: 558
Fat: 38.9g
Saturated Fat: 1.5g
Carbs: 3g

Sugar: 0g
Protein: 46.6g

19. Lemon-Pepper Chicken Wings

Preparation Time 10 m
Cooking Time 20 m
4 Serves

Ingredients:

- Cooking oil
- 1 teaspoon onion powder
- ½ cup all-purpose flour
- 8 whole chicken wings
- Juice of ½ lemon
- ½ teaspoon garlic powder
- Salt
- Pepper
- ¼ cup low-fat buttermilk

Method:
Place the wings in a sealed plastic bag. Drizzle the wings with the lemon juice. Season the wings with the garlic powder, onion powder, and salt and pepper to taste. Seal the bag. Shake thoroughly to combine the seasonings and coat the wings. Pour the buttermilk and the flour into separate bowls large enough to dip the wings. Spray the oven rack/basket with cooking oil. One at a time, dip the wings in the buttermilk and then the flour. Place the wings in the oven rack/basket. It is okay to stack them on top of each other. Spray the wings with cooking oil, being sure to spray the bottom layer. Place the tray rack on the middle shelf of the Air fryer oven. Set temperature to 360°F and cook for 5

minutes. Remove the basket and shake it to ensure all of the pieces will cook fully. Return the basket to the Air fryer oven and continue to cook the chicken. Repeat shaking every 5 minutes until a total of 20 minutes has passed. Cool before serving. Enjoy!

Nutrition:
Calories: 347
Fat: 12g
Protein:46g
Fiber:1g

20. Air Fryer Chicken Parmesan

Preparation Time 5 m
Cooking Time 9 m
4 Serves

Ingredients:

- 8-ounce chicken breasts
- 1 tbsp. melted ghee
- tbsp. gluten-free seasoned breadcrumbs
- ½ C. keto marinara

- tbsp. mozzarella cheese
- tbsp. grated parmesan cheese

Method:
Ensure air fryer is preheated to 360 degrees. Spray the basket with olive oil. Mix parmesan cheese and breadcrumbs together. Melt ghee. Brush melted ghee onto the chicken and dip into breadcrumb mixture. Place coated chicken in the air fryer and top with olive oil. Set temperature to 360°F, and set time to 6 minutes. Cook 2 breasts for 6 minutes and top each breast with a tablespoon of sauce and 1½ tablespoons of mozzarella cheese. Cook another 3 minutes to melt the cheese. Keep cooked pieces warm as you repeat the process with remaining breasts. Enjoy!

Nutrition:
Calories 251
Fat 10g
Protein 31g
Sugar 0g

21. Creamy chicken casserole

Preparation Time 10 m
Cooking Time 45 m
6 Serves

Ingredients:

Chicken and mushroom casserole:

- garlic cloves, minced
- 1 cup all-purpose flour
- 1 medium onion, diced
- 1/2 lbs. (1133.98g) Chicken breasts, cut into strips
- 1 1/2 teaspoon salt
- 1/4 teaspoon black pepper
- tablespoon olive oil
- 1-lb. (453.592g) White mushrooms, sliced

Sauce:

- 1 cup half and half cream
- tablespoon unsalted butter
- tablespoon all-purpose flour
- 1 1/2 cups chicken broth
- 1 tablespoon lemon juice

Method:
Butter a casserole dish and toss in chicken with mushrooms and all the casserole

ingredients. Prepare the sauce in a suitable pan. Add butter and melt over moderate heat. Stir in flour and whisk well for 2 minutes, then pour in milk, lemon juice, and cream. Mix well and pour milk this sauce over the chicken mix in the casserole dish. Press "power button" of air fry oven and turn the dial to select the "bake" mode. Press the time button and again turn the dial to set the cooking time to 45 minutes. Now push the temp button and rotate the dial to set the temperature at 350 degrees f. Once preheated, place the casserole dish inside and close its lid. Serve warm. Enjoy!

Nutrition:
Calories 409
Fat 50.5 g
Cholesterol 58 mg
Sodium 463 mg
Carbs 9.9 g
Fiber 1.5 g
Protein 29.3 g

22. Chicken fajita skewers

Preparation Time 10 m
Cooking Time 8 m
2 Serves

Ingredients:

- 1 teaspoon paprika
- 1 red bell pepper, cut into squares
- 1 teaspoon parsley flakes
- 1 lb. (453.592g) Chicken breasts, diced
- 1 tablespoon lemon juice
- 1 teaspoon chili powder
- 1 teaspoon cumin
- 1 orange bell pepper, cut into squares
- tablespoon olive oil
- 1 teaspoon garlic powder
- 1 large red onion, cut into squares
- 1 teaspoon salt
- 1 teaspoon ground black pepper
- 1 teaspoon oregano

Method:

Toss chicken and veggies with all the spices and seasoning in a bowl. Alternatively, thread them on skewers and place these skewers in the air fryer basket. Press "power button" of air fry oven and turn the dial to select the "air fry" mode. Press the time button and again turn the dial to set the cooking time to 8 minutes. Now push the temp button and rotate the dial to set the temperature at 360 degrees f. Once preheated, place the baking dish inside and close its lid. Flip the skewers when cooked halfway through then resume cooking. Serve warm. Enjoy!

Nutrition:
Calories 392
Fat 16.1 g
Cholesterol 231 mg
Sodium 466 mg
Carbs 13.9g
Fiber 0.9g
Protein 48 g

23. Italian Seasoned Chicken Tenders

Preparation Time 10 m
Cooking Time 10 m
2 Serves

Ingredients:

- 1 tsp sea salt
- 1 tsp paprika
- 1/2 tsp pepper
- 2 eggs, lightly beaten
- 1 1/2 lbs. chicken tenders
- 1/2 tsp onion powder
- 1/2 tsp garlic powder
- 1 tsp Italian seasoning
- 2 tbsp ground flax seed
- 1 cup almond flour

Method:
Preheat the air fryer to 400 F. Season chicken with pepper and salt. In a medium bowl, whisk eggs to combine. In a shallow dish, mix together almond flour, all seasonings, and flaxseed. Dip chicken into the egg then coats with almond flour mixture and place on a plate. Spray air fryer basket with cooking spray. Place half chicken tenders in air fryer basket and cook for 10 minutes. Turn halfway through. Cook remaining chicken tenders using same steps. Serve. Enjoy!

Nutrition:
Calories 315
Fat 21 g
Carbs 12 g
Sugar 0.6 g
Protein 17 g
Cholesterol 184 mg

24. Teriyaki Chicken

Preparation Time 10 m
Cooking Time 20 m
6 Serves

Ingredients:

- 2 tbsp green onion, sliced
- 6 chicken drumsticks
- 1 cup keto teriyaki sauce
- 1 tbsp sesame seeds, toasted

Method:
Add chicken and teriyaki sauce into the large zip-lock bag. Shake well and place in the refrigerator for 1 hour. Preheat the air fryer to 360 F. Add marinated chicken drumsticks into the air fryer basket and cook for 20 minutes. Shake basket twice. Garnish with green onion and sesame seeds. Serve. Enjoy!

Nutrition:
Calories 165
Fat 7 g
Carbs 7 g
Sugar 6 g
Protein 16 g
Cholesterol 65 mg

25. Crispy & Juicy Whole Chicken

Preparation Time 10 m
Cooking Time 60 m
8 Serves

Ingredients:

- 1 1/2 tsp salt
- 1 tsp paprika
- 1 tsp dried basil
- 5 lbs. chicken, wash and remove giblets
- 1/2 tsp onion powder
- 1/2 tsp pepper
- 1 tsp dried oregano

Method:
Preheat the air fryer to 360 F. Mix together all spices and rub over chicken. Place chicken into the air fryer basket. Make sure the chicken breast side down. Cook chicken for 30 minutes then turn to another side and cook for 30 minutes more. Slice and serve. Enjoy!

Nutrition:
Calories 430
Fat 8.6 g
Carbs 0.5 g
Sugar 0.1 g
Protein 82.3 g

Cholesterol 218 mg

26. Thai Chicken with Bacon

Preparation Time 50 m
Cooking Time 20 m
2 Serves

Ingredients:

- 1/2 cup parmesan cheese, grated
- 1 (2-inch piece ginger, peeled and minced
- 1/2 cup coconut milk
- 4 rashers smoked bacon
- 2 chicken filets
- 1/2 teaspoon coarse sea salt
- 1/4 teaspoon black pepper, preferably freshly ground
- 1 teaspoon garlic, minced
- 1 teaspoon black mustard seeds
- 1 teaspoon mild curry powder

Method:
Start by preheating your air fryer to 400 degrees f. Add the smoked bacon and cook in the preheated air fryer for 5 to 7 minutes. Reserve. In a mixing bowl, place the chicken fillets, salt, black pepper, garlic, ginger, mustard seeds, curry powder, and milk. Let it marinate in your refrigerator about 30 minutes. In another bowl, place the grated parmesan cheese. Dredge the chicken fillets through the parmesan mixture and transfer them to the cooking basket. Reduce the temperature to 380 degrees f and cook the chicken for 6 minutes. Turn them over and cook for a further 6 minutes. Repeat the process until you

have run out of ingredients. Serve with reserved bacon. Enjoy!

Nutrition:
Calories 612
Fat 20.3 g
Carbs 1.5 g
Sugar 0 g
Protein 45.2 g
Cholesterol 139 mg

27. Old-Fashioned Chicken Drumettes

Preparation Time 30 m
Cooking Time 22 m
3 Serves

Ingredients:

- 1 heaping tablespoon fresh chives, chopped
- 1 teaspoon garlic paste
- 6 chicken drumettes
- 1/3 cup all-purpose flour
- 1/2 teaspoon ground white pepper
- 1 teaspoon seasoning salt
- 1 teaspoon rosemary
- 1 whole egg + 1 egg white

Method:
Start by preheating your Air Fryer to 390 degrees. Mix the flour with white pepper, salt, garlic paste, and rosemary in a small-sized bowl. In another bowl, beat the eggs until frothy. Dip the chicken into the flour mixture, then into the beaten eggs; coat with the flour mixture one more time. Cook the chicken drumettes for 22 minutes. Serve warm, garnished with chives. Enjoy!

Nutrition:
347 Calories
9.1g Fat
11.3g Carbs

41g Protein
0.1g Sugars

28. Texas Thighs

Preparation Time 10 m
Cooking Time 20 m
8 Serves

Ingredients:

- 2 tablespoons cilantro, chopped
- 8 chicken thighs
- 2 teaspoons Texas BBQ Jerky seasoning

From the Cupboard:

- Salt and ground black pepper, to taste
- 1 tablespoon olive oil

Method:
Preheat air fryer to 380°F (193°C). Spritz the air fryer basket with cooking spray. Arrange the chicken thighs in the air fryer basket, then brush with olive oil on all sides. Sprinkle with BBQ seasoning, salt, and black pepper. Cook for 20 minutes or until the internal temperature of the thighs reaches at least 165°F (74°C). Flip the thighs three times during the cooking time. Remove the chicken thighs from the air fryer basket and serve with cilantro on top. Enjoy!

Nutrition:
Calories: 444
Fat: 33.8g
Carbs: 1.0g

Protein: 31.9g

29. Spicy Turkey Breast

Preparation Time 5 m
Cooking Time 40 m
4 Serves

Ingredients:

- 1 teaspoon red pepper flakes
- 2-pound (907 g) turkey breast
- 2 teaspoons taco seasonings
- 1 teaspoon ground cumin

From the Cupboard:

- Salt and ground black pepper, to taste

Method:
Preheat the air fryer to 350°F (180°C). Spritz the air fryer basket with cooking spray. On a clean work surface, rub the turkey breast with taco seasoning, ground cumin, red pepper flakes, salt, and black pepper. Arrange the turkey in the preheated air fryer and cook for 40 minutes or until the internal temperature of the turkey reads at least 165°F (74°C). Flip the turkey breast halfway through the cooking time. Remove the turkey from the basket. Allow to cool for 15 minutes before slicing to serve. Enjoy!

Nutrition:
Calories: 235
Fat: 5.6g

Carbs: 6.6g
Protein: 37.3g

30. Barbecue Chicken Breast

Preparation Time 15 m
Cooking Time 50 m
4 Serves

Ingredients:

- 1 cup barbecue sauce
- 4 chicken breast fillets
- 2 tablespoons vegetable oil
- Salt and pepper to taste

Method:
Add grill grate to the Ninja Foodi Grill. Close the hood. Choose grill setting. Preheat to medium for 25 minutes. Press start. Brush chicken breast with oil. Sprinkle both sides with salt and pepper. Add chicken and cook for 10 minutes. Flip and cook for another 10 minutes. Brush chicken with barbecue sauce. Cook for 5 minutes. Brush the other side and cook for another 5 minutes. Enjoy!

Nutrition:
Calories: 707
Protein: 62.88 g
Fat: 35.61 g
Carbs: 30.21 g

31. Vinegar London Broil Steak

Preparation Time 15 m
Cooking Time 7 m
5 Serves

Ingredients:

- Salt and freshly ground black pepper, to taste
- 2 garlic cloves, minced
- 1 teaspoon onion powder
- 1½ pounds London broil steak, trimmed
- ¼ cup red wine vinegar
- 1 tablespoon olive oil
- 1 tablespoon Worcestershire sauce
- 1-2 teaspoons fresh rosemary, chopped
- 1 teaspoon dried thyme
- 1½ tablespoons spicy mustard

Method:

With a meat mallet, pound each side of steak slightly. In a large plastic, sealable bag, place the remaining ingredients and mix. Place the steak in bag and seal the bag. Shake the bag vigorously to coat well. Refrigerate to marinate for about 2-4 hours. Remove the steak from the bag and set aside at room temperature for about 30 minutes. Arrange the greased "Grill Grate" in the pot of Ninja Foodi Grill. Close the Ninja Foodi Grill with lid and select "Grill" to "Max" to preheat. Press "Start/Stop" to begin preheating. When the display shows "Add Food" open the lid and place the steak onto the "Grill Grate". With your hands, gently press down the steak. Close the Ninja Foodi Grill with lid and set the time for 7 minutes. Press "Start/Stop" to begin cooking. After 4 minutes of cooking, flip the steak. When the cooking time is completed, press "Start/Stop" to stop cooking and open the lid. Place the steak onto a cutting board for about 10-15 minutes before slicing. With a sharp knife, cut the steak into desired sized slices and serve. Enjoy!

Nutrition:
Calories: 344
Fat: 16.9g
Saturated Fat: 5.4g
Carbs: 3g
Sugar: 1.1g
Protein: 42.1g

32. Glazed Pork Tenderloin

Preparation Time 15 m
Cooking Time 20 m
3 Serves

Ingredients:

- 1 pound pork tenderloin
- 1 tablespoon fresh rosemary, minced
- Salt, to taste
- 2 tablespoons red hot sauce
- 2 tablespoons honey
- ¼ teaspoon red pepper flakes, crushed

Method:

In a small bowl, add the hot sauce, honey, rosemary, red pepper flakes and salt and mix well. Brush the pork tenderloin with mixture evenly. Arrange the greased "Crisper Basket" in the pot of Ninja Foodi Grill. Close the Ninja Foodi Grill with lid and select "Air Crisp". Set the temperature to 350 degrees F to preheat. Press "Start/Stop" to begin preheating. When the display shows "Add Food" open the lid and place the pork tenderloin into the "Crisper Basket". Close the Ninja Foodi Grill with lid and set the time for 20 minutes. Press "Start/Stop" to begin cooking. When the cooking time is completed, press "Start/Stop" to stop cooking and open the lid. Place the pork tenderloin onto a cutting board for about 10 minutes before slicing. With a sharp knife, cut the tenderloin into desired sized slices and serve. Enjoy!

Nutrition:
Calories: 264
Fat: 5.6g
Saturated Fat: 1.9g
Carbs: 12.5g
Sugar: 11.6g
Protein: 39.7g

33. Pesto Rack of Lamb

Preparation Time 15 m
Cooking Time 15 m
4 Serves

Ingredients:

- 1 (1½-pound) rack of lamb
- ½ tablespoons honey
- ½ bunch fresh mint 1 garlic clove
- ¼ cup extra-virgin olive oil
- Salt and freshly ground black pepper, to taste

Method:

For pesto: in a blender, add the mint, garlic, oil, honey, salt, and black pepper and pulse until smooth. Coat the rack of lamb with some pesto evenly. Arrange the greased "Crisper Basket" in the pot of Ninja Foodi Grill. Close the Ninja Foodi Grill with lid and select "Air Crisp". Set the temperature to 200 degrees F to preheat. Press "Start/Stop" to begin preheating. When the display shows "Add Food" open the lid and place the rack of lamb into the "Crisper Basket". Close the Ninja Foodi Grill with lid and set the time for 15 minutes. Press "Start/Stop" to begin cooking. While cooking, coat the rack of lamb with the remaining pesto after every 5 minutes. When the cooking time is completed, press "Start/Stop" to stop cooking and open the lid. Place the rack of lamb onto a cutting board for about 10 minutes. Cut the rack into individual chops and serve. Enjoy!

Nutrition:
Calories: 405
Fat: 27.7g
Saturated Fat: 7.1g
Carbs: 2.8g
Sugar: 2.2g
Protein: 34.8g

34. Bacon-Wrapped Beef Tenderloin

Preparation Time 15 m
Cooking Time 12 m
4 Serves

Ingredients:

- Salt and freshly ground black pepper, to taste
- 8 bacon strips
- 4 (8-ounce) center-cut beef tenderloin filets
- 2 tablespoons 0live oil, divided

Method:

Wrap 2 bacon strips around the entire outside of each beef filet. With toothpicks, secure each filet. Coat each wrapped filet with oil and sprinkle with salt and black pepper evenly. Arrange the "Grill Grate" in the pot of Ninja Foodi Grill. Close the Ninja Foodi Grill with lid and select "Grill" to preheat. Press "Start/Stop" to begin preheating. When the display shows "Add Food" open the lid and place the wrapped tenderloin onto the "Grill Grate". Close the Ninja Foodi Grill with lid and set the time for 12 minutes. Press "Start/ Stop" to begin cooking. After 6 minutes of cooking, flip the tenderloin. When the cooking time is completed, press "Start/Stop" to stop cooking and open the lid. Transfer the tenderloin onto a platter for about 10 minutes before serving. With a sharp knife, cut the tenderloin into desired sized slices and serve. Enjoy!

Nutrition:
Calories: 841

Fat: 52g
Saturated Fat: 16.9g
Carbs: 0.8g
Sugar: 1g
Protein: 87.1g

35. Lemony Flank Steak

Preparation Time 15 m
Cooking Time 12 m
6 Serves

Ingredients:

- Salt and freshly ground black pepper, to taste
- 2 tablespoons olive oil
- 1 teaspoon red chili powder
- 2 pounds flank steak
- 3 tablespoons fresh lemon juice
- 3 garlic cloves, minced

Method:

In a large bowl, add all the ingredients except for steak and mix well. Add the flank steak and coat with the marinade generously. Refrigerate to marinate for 24 hours, flipping occasionally. Arrange the steak into a greased baking pan. Arrange the greased "Grill Grate" in the pot of Ninja Foodi Grill. Close the Ninja Foodi Grill with lid and select "Grill" to "High" to preheat. Press "Start/Stop" to begin preheating. When the display shows "Add Food" open the lid and place the steak onto the "Grill Grate". With your hands, gently press down the steak. Close the Ninja Foodi Grill with lid and set the time for 12 minutes. Press "Start/Stop" to begin cooking. Flip the steak once halfway through. When the cooking time is completed, press "Start/Stop" to stop cooking and open the lid. Place the steak onto a cutting board for about 10-15 minutes before slicing. With a sharp knife, cut the roast into desired sized slices and serve. Enjoy!

Nutrition:
Calories: 339
Fat: 17.4g
Saturated Fat: 6g
Carbs: 0.9g
Sugar: 0.2g
Protein: 42.3g

36. Herbed & Spiced Lamb Chops

Preparation Time 10 m
Cooking Time 7 m
2 Serves

Ingredients:

- 4 (4-ounces) lamb chops
- 1 teaspoon dried thyme
- Salt and freshly ground black pepper, to taste
- 1 tablespoon fresh lemon juice
- 1 tablespoon olive oil
- 1 teaspoon dried rosemary
- 1 teaspoon dried oregano
- ½ teaspoon ground cumin
- ½ teaspoon ground coriander

Method:

In a large bowl, mix together the lemon juice, oil, herbs, and spices. Add the chops and coat evenly with the herb mixture. Refrigerate to marinate for about 1 hour. Arrange the greased "Crisper Basket" in the pot of Ninja Foodi Grill. Close the Ninja Foodi Grill with lid and select "Air Crisp". Set the temperature to 390 degrees F to preheat. Press "Start/Stop" to begin preheating. When the display shows "Add Food" open the lid and place the lamb chops into the "Crisper Basket". Close the Ninja Foodi Grill with lid and set the time for 7 minutes. Press "Start/Stop" to begin cooking. Flip the chops once halfway through. When the cooking time is completed, press "Start/Stop" to stop cooking and open the lid. Transfer the chops onto a platter and top with the remaining garlic mixture. Serve hot. Enjoy!

Nutrition:
Calories: 491
Fat: 24g
Saturated Fat: 7.1g
Carbs: 1.9g
Sugar: 0.2g
Protein: 64g

37. Steak and Mushroom Gravy

Preparation Time 15 m
Cooking Time 15 m
4 Serves

Ingredients:

- Tablespoons vegetable oil
- 1/2 teaspoon onion powder
- 1/3 cup flour
- Cubed steaks
- 2 large eggs

- 1/2 dozen mushrooms
- Tablespoons unsalted butter
- Tablespoons black pepper
- 2 tablespoons salt
- 1/2 teaspoon garlic powder
- 1/4 teaspoon cayenne powder
- 1 1/4 teaspoons paprika
- 1 1/2 cups whole milk

Method:
Mix 1/2 flour and a pinch of black pepper in a shallow bowl or on a plate. Beat 2 eggs in a bowl and mix with a pinch of salt and pepper. In another shallow bowl, mix the other half of the flour with pepper to taste, garlic powder, paprika, cayenne, and onion powder. Chop the mushrooms and reserve. Squeeze the fillet into the first bowl of flour, then dip it into the egg and then press the fillet into the second bowl of flour until completely covered. Place on the oven rack/basket. Place the rack on the middle shelf of the Smart Air Fryer. Set the temperature to 360 ° F and set the time to 15 minutes by turning it halfway. While the steak is cooking, heat the butter over medium heat and add the mushrooms to the stir-fry. Add 4 tablespoons of flour and pepper to the skillet and mix until there are no lumps of flour. Mix in whole milk and simmer. Enjoy!

Nutrition:
Calories 442
Fat 27 g
Protein 32 g
Fiber 2.3 g

38. Asian Inspired Sichuan Lamb

Preparation Time 5 m
Cooking Time 10 m
4 Serves

Ingredients:

- 1 handful fresh cilantro, chopped
- 1 tablespoon light soy sauce
- 2 green onions, chopped
- 1 ½ tablespoons cumin seed (do not use ground cumin)
- 1 teaspoon Sichuan peppers or ½ teaspoon cayenne
- 2 tablespoons vegetable oil
- 1 tablespoon garlic, peeled and minced
- 2 red chili peppers, seeded and chopped (use gloves)
- ¼ teaspoon granulated sugar
- ½ teaspoon salt
- 1 pound lamb shoulder, cut in ½ to 1-inch pieces

Method:
Turn on the burner to medium-high on the stove and heat up a dry skillet. Pour in the cumin seed and Sichuan peppers or cayenne and toast until fragrant. Turn off the burner and set aside until they are cool. Grind them in a grinder or mortar and pestle. In a large bowl that will contain the marinade and the lamb, combine the vegetable oil, garlic, soy sauce, chili peppers, granulated sugar, and salt. Pour in the cumin/pepper combination and mix well. Using a fork, poke holes in the lamb all over the top and bottom. Place the lamb

in the marinade, cover, and refrigerate. You can also use a closeable plastic bag. Preheat the air fryer to 360 degrees for 5 minutes. Spray the basket with cooking spray. Remove the lamb pieces from the marinade with tongs or slotted spoon and place them in the basket of the air fryer in a single layer. You may need to do more than 1 batch. Cook for 10 minutes, flipping over 1 halfway through. Make sure the lamb's internal temperature is 145 degrees F with a meat thermometer. Put on a serving platter and repeat with the rest of the lamb. Sprinkle the chopped green onions and cilantro over top, stir and serve. Enjoy!

Nutrition:
Calories 142
Fat 7 g
Protein 17 g
Fiber 4 g

39. Barbecue Flavored Pork Ribs

Preparation Time 5 m
Cooking Time 15 m
6 Serves

Ingredients:

- 1¾ pound pork ribs
- 1 tablespoon Worcestershire sauce
- Freshly ground white pepper, to taste
- ¼ cup honey, divided
- ¾ cup BBQ sauce
- 2 tablespoons tomato ketchup
- 1 tablespoon soy sauce
- ½ teaspoon garlic powder

Method:

In a large bowl, mix together 3 tablespoons of honey and remaining ingredients except for the pork ribs. Refrigerate to marinate for about 20 minutes. Preheat the Air fryer oven to 355 degrees F. Place the ribs in an Air fryer rack/basket. Cook for about 13 minutes. Remove the ribs from the Air fryer oven and coat with remaining honey. Serve hot. Enjoy!

Nutrition:
Calories 376
Fat 20 g

Protein 32 g
Fiber 12 g

40. Juicy Pork Ribs Ole

Preparation Time 10 m
Cooking Time 25 m
4 Serves

Ingredients:

- 1 teaspoon canola oil
- 1 can tomato sauce
- 1 tablespoon cornstarch
- 1 rack of pork ribs
- 1/2 cup low-fat milk

- 1 tablespoon envelope taco seasoning mix
- 1/2 teaspoon ground black pepper
- 1 teaspoon seasoned salt

Method:

Place all ingredients in a mixing dish; let them marinate for 1 hour. Cook the marinated ribs approximately 25 minutes at 390 degrees F. Work with batches. Enjoy!

Nutrition:
Calories 218
Fat 8 g
Protein 11 g
Sugar 1 g

41. Beef skewers with potato salad

Preparation Time 10 m
Cooking Time 25 m
4 Serves

Ingredients:

- 1 ¼ lb. (566.99g) Diced beef
- Juice ½ lemon
- tablespoon olive oil
- 1 garlic clove, crushed

For the salad:

- 1 bunch of mint, chopped
- 1 cucumber, chopped
- potatoes, boiled, peeled and diced
- large tomatoes, chopped
- 1 handful black olives, chopped
- oz. Pack feta cheese, crumbled

Method:
Whisk lemon juice with garlic and olive oil in a bowl. Toss in beef cubes and mix well to coat. Marinate for 30 minutes. Alternatively, thread the beef on the skewers. Place these beef skewers in the air fry basket. Press "power button" of air fry oven and turn the dial to select the "air fryer" mode. Press the time button and again turn the dial to set the cooking time to 25 minutes. Now push the temp button and rotate the dial to set the temperature at 360 degrees

f. Once preheated, place the air fryer basket in the oven and close its lid. Flip the skewers when cooked halfway through then resume cooking. Meanwhile, whisk all the salad ingredients in a salad bowl. Serve the skewers with prepared salad. Enjoy!

Nutrition:
Calories 609
Fat 50.5 g
Cholesterol 58 mg
Sodium 463 mg
Carbs 9.9 g
Fiber 1.5 g
Protein 29.3 g

42. Glazed beef kebobs

Preparation Time 10 m
Cooking Time 20 m
6 Serves

Ingredients:

- 1 cup Worcestershire sauce
- 1 onion, sliced
- 1 tablespoon parsley, chopped
- lb. (453.592g) Beef, cubed
- 1/2 cup olive oil
- 1 lemon, juice only
- cloves garlic, minced
- 1 teaspoon oregano, dried
- 1/4 teaspoon dried thyme
- 1 teaspoon salt
- 1/4 teaspoon black pepper

Method:
Toss beef with the rest of the kebab ingredients in a bowl. Cover the beef and marinate it for 30 minutes. Thread the beef and veggies on the skewers alternately. Place these beef skewers in the air fry basket. Brush the skewers with the Worcestershire sauce. Press "power button" of air fry oven and turn the dial to select the "air fryer" mode. Press the time button and again turn the dial to set the cooking time to 20 minutes. Now push the temp button and rotate the dial to set the temperature at 370 degrees f. Once preheated, place the air

fryer basket in the oven and close its lid. Flip the skewers when cooked halfway through then resume cooking. Serve warm. Enjoy!

Nutrition:
Calories 457
Fat 19.1 g
Cholesterol 262 mg
Sodium 557mg
Carbs 18.9g
Fiber 1.7g
Protein 32.5 g

43. Macadamia Rack of Lamb

Preparation Time 20 m
Cooking Time 32 m
4 Serves

Ingredients:

- 1 egg, beaten
- ¾ cup unsalted macadamia nuts
- 1 tablespoon breadcrumbs
- 1 tablespoon olive oil
- 1 clove garlic, peeled and minced
- 1 ½ to 1 ¾ pound rack of lamb
- Salt and pepper to taste
- 1 tablespoon fresh rosemary, chopped

Method:
Mix together the olive oil and garlic and brush it all over the rack of lamb. Season with salt and pepper. Preheat the air fryer 250 degrees F for 8 minutes. Chop the macadamia nuts as fine as possible and put them in a bowl. Mix in the rosemary and breadcrumbs and set it aside. Beat the egg in another bowl. Dip the rack in the egg mixture to coat completely. Place the rack in the breadcrumb mixture and coat well. Spray the basket of the air fryer using cooking spray and place the rack inside. Cook at 250 degrees for 25 minutes and then increase to 400 and cook another 5 to 10 minutes or until done. Cover with foil paper for 10 minutes, uncover and separate into chops and serve. Enjoy!

Nutrition:
Calories: 321
Fat: 9g
Protein: 12g
Fiber: 8.3g

44. Caramelized Pork Shoulder

Preparation Time 10 m
Cooking Time20 m
8 Serves

Ingredients:

- 2 pound pork shoulder, cut into 1½-inch thick slices
- 1/3 cup soy sauce
- Tablespoons sugar
- 1 tablespoon honey

Method:
Preparing the Ingredients. In a bowl, mix all the ingredients except pork. Add pork and coat with marinade generously. Cover and refrigerate o marinate for about 2-8 hours. Preheat the Air fryer oven to 335 degrees F. Air Frying. Place the pork in an Air fryer rack/basket. Cook for about 10 minutes. Now, set the Air fryer oven to 390 degrees F. Cook for about 10 minutes. Enjoy!

Nutrition:
Calories: 268
Fat: 10g
Protein: 23g
Sugar: 5

45. Air Fried Herb Rack of Lamb

Preparation Time 5 m
Cooking Time 20 m
2 Serves

Ingredients:

- 4 tablespoons olive oil
- 1 tablespoon thyme, dried
- ½ teaspoon pepper
- 1-pound whole rack of lamb
- 2 tablespoons rosemary, dried

- 2 teaspoons garlic, minced
- ½ teaspoon salt

Method:
Wash the lamb and pat dry. In a mixing bowl, mix all the herbs along with olive oil and keep it aside. Rub the herb mixture over the lamb rack and coat it thoroughly. Place the lamb in the air fryer basket and put it in the inner pot of Instant Pot Air Fryer. Close the crisp lid and set the temperature at 360° F in the AIR FRY mode. Set the timer for 10 minutes. Press START to begin the cooking. Halfway through the cooking, open the crisp lid and flip the lamb for even cooking. After flipping, close the crisp lid, so that the appliance can automatically resume cooking for the remaining period. Once done, remove it from the air fryer and serve hot. Enjoy!

Nutrition:
Calories: 614
Fat: 46.7g
Carbs: 3g
Protein: 47g

46. Easy Air Fryer Pork Chops

Preparation Time 10 m
Cooking Time 20 m
4 Serves

Ingredients:

- Olive cooking oil spray
- ½ teaspoon ground black pepper
- 2 tablespoon olive oil, extra-virgin
- 5 ounces (4 pieces) pork chops, center-cut
- ½ cup parmesan cheese, grated
- 1 teaspoon parsley, dried
- 1 teaspoon ground paprika
- 1 teaspoon garlic powder
- 1 teaspoon salt

Method:
Wash pork chops and pat dry. Using a mixing bowl, combine the parmesan cheese, pepper, parsley, salt, garlic powder, and paprika. Coat the pork chops with the olive oil and then dredge them in the parmesan mixture one by one and place it on a plate. Spritz cooking oil in the air fryer basket and place in the inner pot of the Instant Pot Air Fryer. Place these chops in the air fryer basket in batches. Close the crisp lid. Under the ROAST mode, select the timer for 25 minutes. The temperature by default will remain at 400°F. Press START to begin the cooking. Flip it halfway through for even cooking. Once the cooking over, transfer the pork chop on a cutting board and let it rest for about 5

minutes before you slice and serve. Enjoy!

Nutrition:
Calories 305
Carbs: 1.5g
Fat 16.6g
Protein: 35.3g

47. Chopped Creamy Pork

Preparation Time 15 m
Cooking Time 30 m
6 Serves

Ingredients:

- Salt and black pepper to taste
- 1 tablespoon of olive oil
- 1-1/2 cup of sour cream
- 2 lbs. of pork meat (boneless and cubed)
- 2 yellow onions (chopped)
- 2 tablespoon of Dill (chopped)
- Sweet paprika - 2 tablespoon of
- 1 garlic clove (minced)
- 3 cup of chicken stock
- 2 tablespoons of white flour

Method:
Mix pork with salt, pepper and oil in a pan that fits into your air fryer. Toss well to coat before moving to your air fryer and cook at a temperature of 360 °F, for 7 minutes. Pour some onion, garlic, stock, paprika, flour, sour cream and dill. Toss well to coat and cook at a temperature of 370 °F for another 15 minutes. Divide among different plates and serve immediately. Enjoy!

Nutrition:
Calories: 300

Fat: 4
Carbs: 26
Protein: 34

48. Vegetable Beef Soup

Preparation Time 15 m
Cooking Time 63 m
8 Serves

Ingredients:

- 1 bay leaf (remove after cooking is complete)
- 4 1/2 cups beef broth/ stock
- 1 can diced tomatoes (14.5 ounces)
- 1 pound diced beef (package will often say stew meat)
- 1/2 teaspoon garlic powder (to season the beef - omit if using leftover pot roast)
- 1/2 medium yellow onion, diced
- 2 celery stalks, diced
- 1 cup diced carrots
- Cooking spray or olive oil
- 1/2 teaspoon dried oregano
- Salt and pepper to taste
- 2 cups frozen corn kernels
- 1 cup frozen green beans
- 2 cups diced potatoes

Method:
Preheat the Instant Pot, and spray the pot with cooking spray (or olive oil, if preferred). Add the meat to the pot with garlic powder; salt and pepper generously, and brown for about 3 to 4 minutes. Add the onions, celery and

carrots, and cook for another 3 to 4 minutes. Turn off the pot, and add all other ingredients. Put on the lid, lock it and set to manual high pressure for 8 minutes. (It will take a while to come to pressure with such a full pot, FYI. Mine took 22 minutes.). After the cooking time is complete, allow the pressure to release naturally (without using the quick release lever). Mine took about 25 minutes, FYI. If your pot is still pressurized at 25 minutes, go ahead and quick release any remaining pressure. Remove bay leaf, and serve. Enjoy!

Nutrition:
Calories: 179
Fat: 3g
Carbs: 20g
Protein: 18g

49. Wine Soaked Pork Kebobs

Preparation Time 10 m
Cooking Time 20 m
6 Serves

Ingredients:

- 2 garlic cloves, crushed
- 2 teaspoon dried oregano
- 2 ¼ lbs. (1020.583g) Pork shoulder, diced
- 1/3 cup avocado oil
- ½ cup red wine
- Zest and juice 2 limes

Method:
Whisk avocado oil, red wine, oregano, lime juice, zest, and garlic in a suitable bowl. Toss in pork cubes and mix well to coat. Marinate for 30 minutes. Alternatively, thread the pork, onion, and bread on the skewers. Place these pork skewers in the air fry basket. Press "power button" of air fry oven and turn the dial to select the "air fryer" mode. Press the time button and again turn the dial to set the cooking time to 20 minutes. Now push the temp button and rotate the dial to set the temperature at 370 degrees f. Once preheated, place the air fryer basket in the oven and close its lid. Flip the skewers when cooked halfway through then resume cooking. Serve warm. Enjoy!

Nutrition:
Calories 237

Fat 19.8 g
Cholesterol 10 mg
Sodium 719 mg
Carbs 5.1 g
Fiber 0.9 g
Protein 37.8 g

50. Pork Kebab Tacos

Preparation Time 10 m
Cooking Time 20 m
6 Serves

Ingredients:

- Salt, to taste
- Pork kebabs
- 2 lbs. (907.185g) Pork loin chops, diced
- 1 large onion, squares

For the wrap:

- 1 1/2 cups romaine lettuce, chopped
- 6 burrito wraps
- 1/4 cup onions, sliced
- 1/2 cup tomatoes, sliced

Method:
Toss pork and onion with salt in a bowl to season them. Thread the pork and onion on the skewers alternately. Place these pork skewers in the air fry basket. Press "power button" of air fry oven and turn the dial to select the "air fryer" mode. Press the time button and again turn the dial to set the cooking time to 20 minutes. Now push the temp button and rotate the dial to set the temperature at 370 degrees f. Once preheated, place the air fryer basket in the oven and close its lid. Flip the skewers when cooked halfway through then resume cooking. Place the warm burrito wrap on the serving plates. Divide the

tortilla ingredients on the tortillas and top them with pork kebabs. Serve warm. Enjoy!

Nutrition:
Calories 392
Fat 16.1 g
Cholesterol 231 mg
Sodium 466 mg
Carbs 3.9 g
Fiber 0.9 g
Protein 48 g

Don't miss out!

Visit the website below and you can sign up to receive emails whenever Ann Newman publishes a new book. There's no charge and no obligation.

https://books2read.com/r/B-A-RHUT-DPZZB

BOOKS 2 READ

Connecting independent readers to independent writers.

Also by Ann Newman

Ann Newman Air Fryer Cookbooks

Air Fryer Cookbook: Quick and Easy Recipes to Impress your Family

Air Fryer Cookbook for Beginners: Easy Recipes for Grilling and Frying at Home

Air Fryer Oven Cookbook: Easy and Mouthwatering Recipes for Grilling and Frying at Home

Air Fryer Oven Cookbook for Beginners: Quick and Affordable Recipes for Indoor Frying and Grilling

The Air Fryer Cookbook: Easy and Delicious Recipes for Multicooker, Air Frying, and Pressure Cooking

The Complete Air Fryer Cookbook: Flavorful Recipes to Maximize your Fryer and Multicooker

The Air Fryer Cookbook for Beginners: Quick Beginner Recipes for Baking and Air Frying

The Air Fryer Oven Cookbook: Tasty and Delicious Recipes for Frying, Baking and Grilling Your Dishes

The Air Fryer Oven Cookbook for Beginners: Delicious Recipes with Tips and Tricks to Fry, Roast, Bake and Grill

Simple Air Fryer Cookbook: Healthy Recipes to Bake, Fry or Roast with your Air Fryer

Simple Air Fryer Cookbook for Beginners: Tasty Recipes Anyone Can Fry and Bake at Home

Smart Air Fryer Cookbook: Healthy and Effortless Recipes for People on a Budget

Smart Air Fryer Cookbook for Beginners: Tasty and Delicious Recipes for Easy Meals and a Healthy Diet

The Complete Air Fryer Cookbook for Beginners: Tasty Recipes to Create Healthy Dishes with Air Fryer and Multicooker

Simple Air Fryer Oven Cookbook: Healthy and Friendly Recipes for Frying and Baking at Home

Simple Air Fryer Oven Cookbook for Beginners: Delicious Recipes for Frying, Roasting and Baking for the Whole Family

The Complete Air Fryer Oven Cookbook: Quick and Healthy Homemade Meals Recipes

The Ultimate Air Fryer Cookbook: Delicious Recipes for Baking and Frying at Home

The Ultimate Air Fryer Oven Cookbook: Tasty and Easy to Make Recipes for Any Time of Day

9 798201 920494